The Toga and The Rose

France, 2016.

The Toga and The Rose

To Gina,
Poetry is the breath of life!
Lots of love,
Sheighle x

Sheighle Birdthistle

Copyright © 2014 by Sheighle Birdthistle.

ISBN: Softcover   978-1-4931-4172-2
            eBook   978-1-4931-4173-9

All rights reserved. No part of this book may be reproduced or transmitted in any form or by any means, electronic or mechanical, including photocopying, recording, or by any information storage and retrieval system, without permission in writing from the copyright owner.

This book was printed in the United States of America.

Rev. date: 03/03/2014

To order additional copies of this book, contact:
Xlibris LLC
0-800-056-3182
www.xlibrispublishing.co.uk
Orders@xlibrispublishing.co.uk

Contents

What Beckett's Endgame did to me 9
Poetry 11
Hope 12
Words 13
Hazelwood 14
Even the trees are lonely 15
The Hand of God Gloved 16
Myth 17
Oh Mother Moon 18
Gone 19
The Poppy Fields of France 20
Land of the Sighe 21
Syria 22
Terror 23
Sonnet 46664 24
Walls 25
The Living Dead 27
Starry Night 28
Alexander the Great 29
Son 30
Daughters 31
Four Souls of my Body 32
The Second Starry Night 33
Taste 34
Poet 35
The Sad Child 36
The night before I died 37
Fearful Lovers 38
A Murder of Crows 39
Greece to Google 40
Who Cares for a Breaking Heart on a Starry Night? 41

Colours	43
The Lady	45
Prostituted for Silver	46
Emigrant	47
New Orleans	48
Finale	49
Crisis	50
Lonely Starry Night	51
Wild Horse	52
A Ribbon of Life	53
My Sister	54
Problems	55
No Title	56
The End	57
Gossip	58
Denial	59
Holding Hands	60
A Star has Come for Me	61
The Woman Looks in the Mirror	62
Naked Longing	63
Ways to love?	64
Black Dog Christmas	65
Earth, your dancing place	66
Weird	67
In Memory	69
Easter Sunday	70
War	71
A Vision of Ulster '74	72
Tiananmen Square	73
The Toga and The Rose	74

For Sandy and my family

"I love the bones of you"

What Beckett's Endgame did to me . . .

Restrain me from the stillness of oblivion let me dance instead in the magic ring of imagination hop skip and dance to the music of the earth positing a meaning of existence existence out ranging all other emotions or smileys on a screen pretending to send fondness from me to you from you to me scrap the rubbish and face up to truth in the universe and exist if existence is your problem you are only the sum of your acts if you want to live an existentialist life but me I like words dance and wine and will not make any more excuses as I move through the crazy cycle of life of madness of wonder in the magnificence of the forest of trees the smashing splashing of waves and birdsong singing for me in the darkness of day the brightness of night all mixed up together making me positively exhilarated by this absurd world
Luna Luna
Peach coloured moon
Hangs half way in the sky
Something strange about
The ambience tonight
They drive on and on
A scattering of birds
Come into vision
As they hurry a flight
Pattern towards the
Inviting light of Luna
They drive on
Their direction not clear
On into the night
Landscape changing
From peach to orange
To yellow and red
As tears mist their

View the windscreen
Mists over light
Becomes ever brighter
The hanging moon
Descends lower and
Ever lower in the sky
As they halt and on foot
Make their way to the moon
Grappling with vines
With trees with mountains
Howling at the moon for
Solace for quiet for help
They do not accept their
Own madness as all is
Scrambled on the planet
That holds beauty in thrall
That screams in tenor tones
To advance advance
They move on and on
They see the new horizon
As Luna wanes still
Hanging half crooked
As they feel frozen
In a new hemisphere
Of existence sickly
Pointing at the moon
A moon that slides
Down from a sky ablaze
With other things like stars
And dreams and words
They come
To a slow slow stop.

Poetry

I found something in the garden.
Sitting on a bench soaking hot
Drenched in a sense of awe.
Afternoon light, bright beams
Filtered by strands of green
Different shades of green.
Fine, dark and shrouded shadows
All green, hanging, creeping,
Lush in arrogant tresses.
Walled garden safe and silent
Only the thrilling fountain
Drip feeding my thirst.
It happened that day
I found something in the garden.

Hope

Hope is a four lettered word
Beautiful to have if you have it.
A mass of indescribable terror if not
Taken and shaken and set apart
From the heart and spirit
She saw the boat. Escape.
Or maybe a way home.
She saw the boat. Food.
Fish from the deep sea.
She saw the boat. People.
Singing raw anthems.
She sees the boat. Now
She knows the meaning
Of hope.

Words

Here is the empty page
this is me.
Take it and write on it
your shallow love is ink
spluttering and staining
my sheets with your love.
Love! Your need satisfied
I lie here knowing
that you will go back to her.
Ink dries and leaves a history
you are tearing at my insides
I leave my desire and dignity
in an inkwell.

Hazelwood

I walked into the hazel patch
And plucked a bough from the bush
Inhaled the scent of sorrow
In that place of hush and secret.
Ordered by a strange power
With bough outstretched,
To ramble over fertile green
Over bog of rich dark turf
Alive in its death shell, warmly
Nourishing the perfection
Embalmed within its depths.
As moonlight crept from clouds
And crows cawed their way home
To nests in high dark trees,
Cows lowed in meadows
That now seemed ominous.
Darkness clawing at my soul
That strange power urged
Me onwards to a place
Where stones heaped on stone
Rose in a circle
A wide wide circle.
Gossamer fog fell
As I fell to my knees
And prayed and scourged
My innermost soul
For understanding.

Even the trees are lonely

Even the trees are lonely.
Waking on a still, bright day
Hope gnawing slightly

She sees from her room
The russet and gold leaves
Falling like tears

She tries to ingest her cry
It swells like the buds
She may not know,

When spring cracks
Nature's desire
To fulfil its destiny.

Turning away
She sleeps
Perhaps forever.

The Hand of God Gloved

A life that should have been yellow, coloured grey.
Cotton fields blazing sun and laughter
Singing in the cloisters like angels
The man swung his belt and blasted
The beauty from all time
As innocence lost its rhyme
They found a new reality.
A life that should have been yellow, coloured grey
Black skin the only sin
Eyes dark as the blood soaked earth.
As the light dimmed and died
The singing in the cloisters of demons
Rattled the chains
Of hunger and thirst
A life that should have been yellow, coloured grey
Is now black.
The hand of god gloved.

I walked into a meadow
And asked a man for gold
He said that I was ugly
And that I should be sold
For half a pint of nothing.
A life that should have been yellow, coloured grey.
I was the Devil's Agent, he said. He took the child away.
The well is deep. How harsh the sleep
There is no anodyne for pain
The constant gnawing strain
For a life that should have been yellow, coloured grey.
The hand of god still gloved.

Myth

Each day he urges his dumper, onward
upwards, up the hill, filling the bucket
with rocks and trying, trying, to distil
an aura of nonchalance.
Up, up the hill he goes
down again they fall.
The bucket scoops and fills and fills.
He has never heard of Sisyphus.

Oh Mother Moon

How do you sing the song of life?
When you have not even lived
There is no direction. Only longing
For two arms reaching eager to warm you
Happy to dance with you
Never knowing the steps
Both out of tune
Both out of step.
Clinging to a time
Past as if present.
Oh mother moon.

Gone

She danced a sharp fandango
and knew the tango in her brain
unslaked by rain was death
to the lonely breath of her soul.
Step by step, curving the hips
pursed lips inching towards passion
no sense of the rational informing
the morning after
the night before.
Suspended with delight close to stars
one twinkling with super light. A fantasy.
Star two spiralling to oblivion. Destiny.
My choice to make
a break from crashing
stress lines flashing
bad words lashing
memories rehashing
love lacking
bags packing.
Gone.

The Poppy Fields of France

The fields are full of poppies; my heart bleeds
Deep in my field of dreams, in my sad soul,
They stretch on and on. Far away
I see wooden crosses of men and boys
Slain on fields of green, turned poppy red
With blood of the ordered man.
The stem of the delicate flower
Is strong, as the obedient soldier
It sways in the breeze, persisting.
Can you hear the cry of the dead?
Listen! The scream of the living
Tells of the greatness of survival
The slaughter of death.
Of the longing to be home
To see in the fields, the poppies
Growing wild and free.

Land of the Sighe

We are a strange lot us Irish
The O'Rahilly wrote "thou art not
conquered yet dear land."
We are a strange lot pushing forward
But forever looking back.
Rooted in the land of the Sighe
We danced to the whisper of wings
And revelled in the faery fort.
One step forward one step back
Kneeling to a supernatural presence
Accepting a Host, or a host of fairies
With the same enduring superstition
That same notion informing our beginning.
Trees apples and demons
And the languid woman devouring
The creation and transforming
The garden into a wilderness.
"Thou art not conquered yet dear land."

Syria

The trees that form the arches
Over the road I am travelling
Reach towards each other like lovers
Grasping at each other like clasping hands.
The falling leaves drop like huge tears of sorrow
On the poppies scattered at their roots.
Poppies, symbol of fallen dead glow red
Short growth, a stunted life span
Beneath a starry sky of madness
Or the full moon of pulling tides.
Birdsong is dulled by the dying cry of Syria
Man on man, on woman, on child
Wreaking a murderous counter revolution.
Who hears the cry of the dying?
Who hears the cry of the bewildered?
A setting aside of a problem that is not ours
Is setting aside our humanity as we rejoin
The kingdom of the animal; unable to think, to speak
Or show compassion for difference

The raging passion of a red hunger
Cannot be sated by bloodshed.

Terror

Yesterday is today. Today is tomorrow.
Sitting shackled soils the soul.

Now I am a freedom fighter
Fighting for my own existence.

Five years ago shopping for spice
At my village market. I was marked.

Three masked men, strangers, ruined me
They did not show their faces. Cowards.

No smiles light my life no love warms me
In this dead man's land of no return

I have to dig deep into my heart and soul
To find reason a god and a vestige of hope.

If I were Christian I would have to forgive these men of violence
But now it is my need to retaliate that keeps me breathing.

Sonnet 46664

Each day like the day before and days to come
Robben Island adrift lacking humanity
Hearts and spirits turned away from sun
Ordered by the whitewashed insanity
Of a system that could not see beauty
In the different shades of mankind's skin
But considered instead control its duty
Murdering of self without and within
"Free Nelson Mandela" became the loudest cry
White doves wrote it in the African sky
Sanctions the conscience of capitalism
Coloured in a swath of idealism
His dream must go on become true reality
As he sleeps in a warm rest for eternity.

Walls

She dreamed of walls
Walls of all kinds
Keeping in
Keeping out.
Countries divided
Cities cut in two.
Angelique the brave
Resisted the obvious
Salome danced.
Out came the unicorn
Thrilling the region
Creating belief
As Caesar strummed
His guitar in grief.
Honey flows
Bees are happy
Rivers shimmer
Under bridges
Escaping walls.
She dreamed of walls
Graffiti painting words
She dreamed of walls
Pressed to her lover
As he kissed her breast.
Walls walls walls.
No words spoken
Walls to climb
To break down
Walls to adorn
To mount joyfully
Walls? Walls?
China. Berlin. Jerusalem
My back yard

Your garden
Your house
My house.
Walls. Walls.
Television. Radio.
Internet. No kisses
No hugs, no handshakes.
No communication.
Not wailing walls
Screaming walls. Walls.

The Living Dead

Living dead move like ghosts through empty halls.
Unseen, seeking a voice and a place to rest.
Ragged edges of existence numb the space
Occupied by the here and now; the neverland.
Dust as dust whirling beyond recognition
Resting at last in the lush green grass of France.

Starry Night

I lie under a sky ablaze with stars and I wonder
If the stars were words, what would be written
And who would write?
Little pools of light reaching out
And reaching to us, light years away.
Words, stars, words blending
And rending us poets rigid with wonder
As we ponder.
Mixing and twisting our words
To match the moment, forgetting
That our words are the stars
That give light and life to our being.
As I lie here the stars begin to fall from the sky
In a free fall beauty
I try to catch my words to feel the light
To know a sense of wonder.
But something draws me to a stop.
A full stop.
No words.
World of stars you make me ablaze within the cold.
Cold. When there are neither words nor stars.

Alexander the Great

If, I could write like them;
The poets of days gone by
You might contemplate my words
And consider them of worth.
I pay thee homage my love
My kind and passionate man
Who watches over me with eyes
Of Atlantic blue.
Your warm love engulfs me
When I am in that dark and lonely place
And I reach to touch your saddened face.
But today, we will dance the Tango
Close, in the dance of love.

Son

He sent me a text
Loaded with love and feeling
'Mum remember we are with you
We can talk when you want to.'
Life gets in the way
Distance blurs meaning.
That firstborn is now a man
Upright strong and good
His eyes filled with love
Regard his own, growing
Strong as young oaks.
But when he takes my hand in his
And kisses my cheek
He is my boy.

Daughters

I feel their breath on my skin
They are my morning sun,
My evening moon
The scent of flowers
And birdsong.
Nature's best and
Nature's cloudy days.
They are music and poetry
Dervish dancers
Swirling through time.
And wise, wild women!
They move with beauty
Commune with the earth
And spirituality.
They fish wisdom
From the seas of mortality
Holding hands together
They hold mine.
I love the bones of them.

Four Souls of my Body

Then and now gently, in the storm of life.
We love each other, in different ways
Tempests and gentle torrents
Flowing like angels' wings
Touching, and smiling at each other's jokes.
But time rests long on a mother's shoulders
It is gossamer to the young.
I remember laughter strong as the west wind
As I grapple with the Mistral,
Amid olive groves and vines that curl
Like my babies' fingers 'round mine
When they suckled. As I need wine
To quench my longing for my children
On Mother's Day, and every day.

The Second Starry Night

My starry night is here again
As I sense that veil, that fatigue.
The stars predict tomorrow
Their light will then arrive
To shed gloss on our today.
What about the interim
The budding trees the fledgling birds. Me?
Turquoise blue skies,
Rounded stones in streams
And candyfloss clouds
Telling of a tempest to come.
Come to me, come to us
You beautiful star of revelation.

Taste

The lonely man sits in the corner shelling peas
Each empty pod is like the useless kisses
That she stole from him with raging passion.
So lovely a hunger satisfied, red hot
Chilli pepper burns on the tongue of desire.
He tastes a freshly podded pea. It's not the same.

Poet

He tried to hide himself for the simple reason
that he could not accept the self that he found
lurking in the shadows.
Metaphor was his mask he wore many
both Tragedy and Comedy fitted him well
he sat in a corner and thought; there is no one
left in the world.
It is cold and wild here in my mind
Sun has stopped shining
and the only sound is wind.

The Sad Child

My beautiful child, do not weep.
Let me take your burden
Of sorrows on my shoulders.
And so let you run free
And wild once more
Talk to me, do not be frightened.
I love you.
You place your hand in mine,
You cling to me.
I'll always be here for you.
So rest easy, do not be anxious anymore.
My little girl. My woman child.

The night before I died

My body was apain
With pain they were
One thing body
And pain.
Noise I remember
The noise of patients
Making empty
Meaningless sounds
All afraid.
The night before I died
I no longer cared
For Earth's loveliness
Nor craved touch
Then silence
In a ward loud
With existence
As I knew
No more pain.
Lying there
Receiving oil
Of anointment
As I watched
In an ether
Of somewhere
Else
Somehow I
Got my life back.

Fearful Lovers

Does anyone else hear the screaming?
Or is this round noise inside my head?
It fills the space that is my mind and
I ache with the fear and the realisation
That I cannot stop it.
It is a sound and a sensation and a longing.
A longing to be free.
A free spirit a blithe soaring singing spirit
Will I only be free when I am still?

I love the bones of him, she said
But he has a sound within his head
A round and bright and terrible noise
That saps him of his hopes and joys
It fills him with a dread and fear
I cannot hear it, 'though close and near
He does not heed my anguished shout
And in his despair, he locks me out.

A Murder of Crows

We jumped into the deep well
I was looking for love
He wanted water.
Then came a murder of crows
Ready for a slaughter
Squatted round and round
Uttering inane laughter
Found the love I was after
In the madness of his lips
He praised my curving hips
Madness found its level
In that deep deep well.

Greece to Google

Friend Socrates
Welcome to our world
Your rhetoric tells of
Fluctuation and annihilation
Nothing changes.
I am hungry for discourse
You would talk to me
No text, no tweet to cloud the good.
There is no oracle today
Only google
To comment on the wise.
You are the gadfly
For our late Athens
We walk numbed
Pass me more hemlock.

Who Cares for a Breaking Heart on a Starry Night?

It's a breaking heart that reads
Of people and places loved in another time.
A coming home to Israel and not being a Jew
But needing to be. Needing.
Needing to find a homeland.
The Azores island of Flores
Birthed a grandfather
So far from red haired Irish.
But the heart knows something
An intrinsic knowing.
The longing longing
In the waters of the Jordan
As the child was plunged for healing.
The sense of being home
In a land fraught as the body is fraught
Unable to cope.
It's a breaking heart that sees across a room
Chocolate eyes from Syria
And remembers a warring tank
Close to a kibbutz.
Breaking hearts heal. Bodies die.
The spirit of the breaking heart
Hangs like the thread of the boots
Of stealth in the night.
Boots that trample the innocent
Without regret.
Families fixated on formality.
The starry night does not matter tonight.
The stars show too much.
Darkness hides.

Creaking doors scatter the cat that calms.
Words, not from stars
But an evil mouth
Shatter the breaking heart
And its pieces lie soaking
The blood of innocence.
But, in all honesty . . .
Who cares for the breaking heart?

Colours

Yellow is happiness
With light passing through
It becomes bright gold.
Blueness is sadness
A feeling so cold.
If, mixed together,
Colour becomes green
As leaves still strong tell
Of the beauty unseen.
The colours of life
Reflect through a prism
The saw of a dream.

The road not taken is a cliché
That I have taken over and over.
Over the sun, over the moon
One day at a time.
Take a step back and grin
Sandals and a dheblla
A prayer at the mosque
And a getaway prayer.
Pray a rosary and sing
Hari Krishna Hari Krishna.
Oh ye of little faith.
To be or not to be.
I love you.
Love is a red red rose.
Oh to have a little house
Like the little house
On the prairie.
The prairie is awash
With G.M.
And hunger stalks

The world.
The world is now
A smaller place
Where rape is easy
And ego takes flight.
Take my hand
And we will fly away.
I believe in the tooth fairy
And runes and crosses
And people who care.
But who am I?
A woman or a man
Who sheds skin
Like lies and snakes.

The Lady

I have waited for this moment
To guide you to freedom.
I cannot express my feelings so
Full am I with emotion.
Can we now
Begin a new life together?
My name is Burma
Never forget. Burma.
The Generals of fear
Took my identity
They took your freedom
To name me Myanmar.
Never forget; my name is Burma.

Prostituted for Silver

File, ancient poet
Wisdom of ages
Scorn of mediocrity.
With strong wind blowing
High waves flowing
Our file inhaled
Exhaled the breath
Of fairy wonder,
Of thoughts of
Ages past of
Hope for future days.
File, ancient poet
Wisdom of ages
Scorn of mediocrity
Breathe blessings
Of antiquity
On this revered land
Prostituted for silver
As its rivers ran golden
With young and old.

Emigrant

On my Skype screen I touch your photo
I touch your face. No reaction.
Days when we talked there were not
Enough words alive for us to speak
We danced around each sentence
Curving the circumference of our lives.
We settled wars, cured illness, kissed.
Time is only for looking back
Back into a space inhabited warmly
By a passion unchecked, unchanged.
But, that is my side of the story.

New Orleans

Before Katrina
Preservation Hall rocked
In sashay dancing
Hearts romancing
You seemed to sense my soul
Without the rock'n'roll
Tipp tapping away
Jazzing to the sway
Sipping the scent of creole
Loving your chocolate eyes
Longing to believe your lies
As we waited for the storm.

Finale

Another night of terror. Hurt, hurt
He argued with her.
His life half lit. Soul extinguished.
Walk, walk, no one walking
The long mile alone
Wind screaming, his ears on fire
His heart out of tune with reality
Passion thumped him.
Could he do it? He sat to plan.
Count the sleepers. One week, two . . .
The pain would sleep with him.
Finally a good night's sleep
With no waking?

He wakes
The wind screams at him
But he cannot hear.
Woodland releases birds escaping
He begs his psyche
But it is too damaged.
He fills the prescription
Sits in the car. And waits.

Two days pass.
No understanding
He seemed happy
He seemed normal
Everything to live for.
They do not realise
That life is a cliché.

Crisis

It's a small village hiding big lives
Aghast with colour and sound,
Red earth warms the footprint
As green arbours pour
Shelter from the rising sun.
It also rises, day by day
Perfect in structure
Oblivious to the moans of man.
Nature blesses, man curses
The unstructured mind.
The hurting, not knowing
The way to exist.
Who pays the piper?
What pays the piper?
Thirty pieces of silver?
The little person in the village
Of big lives,
Is preparing to go with
The setting sun. The shame.
They sit opposite each other
Counting coins to drink coffee
To keep that aura of sophistication.
So no one will know.
Play music. Keep clean.
Sleep longer each morning
To stay warm.
They read poetry
It is free.
They will be free
If the plan works.

Lonely Starry Night

Where are you my darling stars?
you who give me hope
I stand and watch and wait
and wilt with wishes waning
you are hidden like the clouds of catastrophe,
that claim the substance of
sustaining serenity seamlessly.
The blue moon of reality
realised as the rogue of the realm
shading the starry sky solemn and serene.
Ah wait! My starry night is here again!

Wild Horse

It is the unwise who tries to tame the wild horse.
I am the wild horse who will take you to oblivion
On my back I can carry you to the heights of wonder
And the depths of normality.
It is I who writes the entrails of the world across the night sky
And in the morning ploughs the beauty of the earth.
I am the wild wild horse of the world
Your lover and beloved. Tame me.

A Ribbon of Life

The tree is awake now
And pink flowers
Like buds on young breasts
Shake in the soft breeze
And float like gossamer
To the dry dry earth.
So sweet a vision
Innocent to passing eyes
That delight to see
A ribbon of life, casting
Around and around
In the ever soft breeze.
A river runs by and rounded
Stones, of ages past lie still.
Does this calm you?
Are you drawn into
The lovely moment?
Do you enjoy idyllic days
In the sun, body warm, content?
The girl enjoyed a time,
The girl climbed the tree.
The tree with pink flowers.
Flowers like buds on young breasts
Shaking in the soft breeze.
The girl swam naked in the river
Caressed by the ancient stones
And turned her face to the sun
And howled for the moon.
Then she climbed higher
And commended her clean spirit
To oblivion.

My Sister

In many halls there is a twist
That takes you up, or down
Along a corridor of dreams.
The music senses your approach and relaxes quavering
To the clash of cymbals.
Your brown eyes dance in a head aglow with auburn curls.
Knowing more philosophy than the Oracle as you teach
With wit and wisdom
The way to live a life.
I love the bones of you.

Problems

No excuse left
To explain
The anger
The shame
The fatigue.

No excuses
Sun shines
Rain purifies.

Forgiveness
Has its own
Problems.

No Title

Send her silently to bed, he said, she is a troubled woman
But she sang her song and slipped softly out of her skin.
No way back now, never to scrape her skin with salt
Dreaming of diving into the cold calm canyon alone.
Too late time run out running always running away
To someone from something, tethered to a tree
Not tree hugging hiding in hedgerows hoping
It might be better this time this time?
Time out, time, no time it's time.

The End

It's not normal
This craving to
Cleave to the wind
And take, the shroud
Garment to hide
From the approach
That nears the edge.
Hurting hurting.
Life a pillow
To ease the end.

Who calls the wind
Who answers?
Swift arrows pain
Straight to the heart.
Give me my garment
And let me go.

Gossip

Some people grow like mushrooms
Inhabiting the earth, but
Sullied by their reference
To each other.
Quietly they feed off each other
Until goodness is eroded.
Then they are left
As fodder for the enemy
In an army of ineptitude.
The good are taken to the edge
And turn into obsolete people
Beyond their sell by date.

Denial

Crawling out of the sea
you shed your scales,
your many layers of scales
and left behind your wisdom
of the sea and your knowledge.
Scraping earth to find feet,
you harnessed a new power
and struggled to stand
and hid your first nature
of true beast;
You hacked an education
defined a new you,
clouded your lusts
claimed a new life.
Better you had kept
your origin of beast.
You call yourself priest.

Holding Hands

They gaily skipped into a woodland
Hand in hand no golden band
To regulate their fresh faced passion
Walking dancing glowing, so good
Paradise in a country wood.
A stream trickled beneath red skies
Sun reflected the hope in their eyes.
Then, torn asunder. Hope died
The galloping marauder attacked
Knife in hand he hacked and hacked.
Metaphorically speaking
Secrets secrets leaking.
Raged anger coursed through him
Making knots. Hurting.
A glint in his eyes a passion
Hungry for appeasement.
All rhyme diminished
Happiness finished
They held hands.

A Star has Come for Me

A star has come for me
Its bright busy light
Drips words like droppings
Enriching an earth that
Is barren and bleak.
A star has come for me
A halo happens
All show all bravado
Words, words, words.
A star has come for me
I will go with the star
The star that has come for me.

The Woman Looks in the Mirror

The woman looks in the mirror
she presents herself each morning,
as she searches to invent
the woman she will be today
she drinks from her well of identities.

The woman plucks from the pots of foundation
the colours she will mix to match her mind
and she fixes her base with bland bonding
a fine powder, alabaster white.

The pencilled brows and the pencilled lips
are the frame for the eyes and expression
or, lack of expression?

The eyes are bathed in colour or maybe nude
it depends on who she is, or thinks she is, today.

Naked Longing

He missed a time
meadows were green
with a sheen of delight
from the glow of a
warm sun
morning was an
amazing adventure
long waiting in the night
to encounter her scent
it was perfect this love
obsessively loved him
making loving life a joy
walking in woods afire
in colours like his heart
overflowing not knowing
the why and not caring why
warm cold all wonderful
hunger and thirst slaked
by loving her all of her
arms legs lips one tree
from roots of perfection
springing out of a universe
not understood when
drinking sips of nectar
in the naked flow of a
rippling stream eating
wild strawberries as
summer bees kept
from stinging by laughter
laughter of innocence
he missed her intensity
that look that said yes
or showed the lonely
creature that was her soul
until he caressed enfolded
her and folded her to him.

Ways to love?

There are more ways
of loving
More ways of knowing
How to feel that
Unbelievable passion
That thrills the bones
The essence of
Muscles that support
The sizzling of hotness
When life is good
More ways of believing
That there is
A way out.
More ways to kiss
When love is cold
And arms need
Arms to embrace
There are more
Ways to love . . . .

Black Dog Christmas

Out into the wild woods
Hurrying, forging away
Into another, other
Way of existence
The black dog and I
We will romp together
As only black dogs
And sorry people
Can romp at Christmas.
Head in the sand?
Nose in the air, loud, quiet?
The black dog will decide
Us together, side by side.

Earth, your dancing place

Earth, your dancing place
fixed in his heart, beginnings
rejoicing in your deep red ochre.
Cultures painted in warmth
as he dances
reflect the artist's work.
Spiralling out of control
the dance becomes a poem
screaming in the wilderness.

His whole body goes into scream
sensing the aged existential angst
the corrosive burning of self
Drained through and through
he demands an explanation
and gets none. Down avenues
of revelation, the dead prey
on leaving bad memories
to the living
who scatter themselves
like thunder clouds
booming no forgiveness.
Can retribution cleanse?
Can sorrow be healed?
Through understanding.

Weird

He has jumped into wells
Looking for love.
He has touched the hand
Of god, gloved.
But, where is he now?
No, not god, the man
Who awaits his fix.
No, not drugs
Understanding.
His hair is coming out
No, not him
His hair.
He is trying to harness
The wind
I said the wind,
To take him away.
I want to go with him.

We are lost together
This man and me
In our skin
There is a soakage
Of a long ago
Belief in love.
Where is the wind?
The wind that
Blows softly
To eternity.

A place unknown
Only a reincarnation.
Oh, please,
A release.

Take us to hell
If it is a happy place
To its circle of magic
Or heaven.
Not a hell on earth
Breathe in, breathe out.
Save the last one.

A suffocation of the divine
If there is a divine
As we perceive it.
Hanging a heart
Full of love
Ready to explode
And infiltrate philosophy.
Is there anyone there?
I am because I am?
Oh take me East
And learn to know
The circulation
Of existence.
Existence, I said
Not subsistence.
Bury me near a tree
But above ground.

In Memory

Lapping of water
Leaping at my body
Deep into my soul
A true sense of peace
Of hunger appeased.
Strengthen my back
Teach me to breathe
One breath only.
Give before receiving
Or take me forever . . . please.
A man walks straight into the wood
He begs the gods of the tall trees
To listen to the little white man.
Teach him to breathe one tiny last breath
Strengthen his back show him your grace.
But the great black hole calls, it screams
Come to me I will make you well.
He tries, once more, a deep deep breath
But, he never exhales.

Easter Sunday

A little bird fell from the sky. Hurt.
Its small wings fluttering, weakly
The tiny heart beating against skin.
Skin so fine it barely covered its breast
It lay on the hard so-cold ground, helpless.
Then, a white butterfly swooped
Kissed the bird, flew away
As if to say. It is done.
I put the bird in a box
With cotton wool to warm him
And waited.
Memories
Sun filled Easter morning in Spain
My heart and soul at ease. So sweet.
My teenage children, my beloved
Filling my vista and my heart.
A white dove swoops low to kiss me
Flies away.
I feel a love and a quiet peace.
It grabs and hugs me 'till I gasp.
It was at that moment in time
In another place, my father died.

War

The trees that form the arches
Over the road I am travelling
Reach towards each other like lovers
Grasping at each other like clasping hands.
The falling leaves drop like huge tears of sorrow
On the poppies scattered at their roots.
Poppies, symbol of fallen dead glow red
Short growth, a stunted life span
Beneath a starry sky of madness
Or the full moon of pulling tides.
Birdsong is dulled by the dying cry of Syria
Man on man, on woman, on child
Wreaking a murderous counter revolution.
Who hears the cry of the dying?
Who hears the cry of the bewildered?
A setting aside of a problem that is not ours
Is setting aside our humanity as we rejoin
The kingdom of the animal; unable to think, to speak
Or show compassion for difference
The raging passion of a red hunger
Cannot be sated by bloodshed.

A Vision of Ulster '74

She dreamed of a land so fair
Where fighting and killing were rare
Where her sons could learn to reap and sow
And daily in God's peace could grow

Where little girls could have their fun
Instead of learning to hit and run
From the troops who roam their streets
To protect men when religion meets.

She dreamed this dream as she watched the news
In fifty years she'd kept her views
And was she not right, not to give in?
Sure, to look at a Protestant here was a sin.
Now her dreaming is over, she's an Irish mother
And she knows one man is as good as another
So now she pleads with foe and friend
Help us make this killing end.

Tiananmen Square

Sloe eyed Chinese boys and girls
Youth denied democracy
Born into a way of life
Unknown in the West.
We watch we wait. Weeks.
Then like a pulse bursting
Redness flashed on our television screens
Obscene death on beautiful young bodies. Bleeding.
Red blood, red pouring on red.
Outpouring. Life stilled.

Democracy now is only a word.
They lie dead in Tiananmen Square.

The Toga and The Rose

She wears a toga and in her hair, a rose
She is revered for her beauty and perfect roman nose.
Each day she reaches out to hold him
While plaintively demanding, if she is, still slim
Enough, to wear a toga and in her hair, a rose.
She knows a place you will not want to visit
It is dank and lonely without movement
It stagnates all waters waiting to weep
No place for a toga, and in the hair, a rose.
It is a day, a cliché day, like any day
But she cannot get through
Without her toga and her rose.
Feels taints of lonely status
Too tired to really care
Oh! Let them stare
At my toga and my rose.